WISE CHOICES

WISE CHOICES

A Spiritual Guide to
Making Life's Decisions

MARGARET SILF

BlueBridge

Cover design by Angel Guerra
Cover photography by Corbis
Text design by Jennifer Ann Daddio

Library of Congress Cataloging-in-Publication Data

Silf, Margaret.
Wise choices : a spiritual guide to making life's decisions / Margaret Silf.
p. cm.
ISBN-13: 978-1-933346-04-5
ISBN-10: 1-933346-04-3
1. Choice (Psychology) 2. Decision making. 3. Choice (Psychology)—Religious aspects.
4. Decision making—Religious aspects. I. Title.
BF611.S55 2007
153.8'3—dc22
2006031400

Text copyright © 2004, 2007 Margaret Silf
Original edition published in Great Britain under the title
On Making Choices by Lion Hudson plc, Oxford, England
Copyright © Lion Hudson plc 2004

First published in North America in 2007 by
B l u e B r i d g e
An imprint of
United Tribes Media Inc.
240 West 35th Street, Suite 500
New York, NY 10001

www.bluebridgebooks.com

Printed in the United States of America

1 3 5 7 9 10 8 6 4 2

CONTENTS

INTRODUCTION

Decisions, decisions
—not just half a dozen, but scores, even hundreds of them,
every day.

The range of choices we face in daily life
seems to grow exponentially,
and so does the accompanying stress.

Making choices has become something of a
full-time activity
in an increasingly complex world.
It's a skill that is demanded of us constantly
in our everyday living.

Is it something we can learn to do well?
Or is it just a matter of reacting more or less blindly
to the demands of the moment?

And what can we do to reduce some of the stress
that life's unending choices place upon our time and
our quality of life?

The aim of this book is to help make the task of choosing less stressful, more focused, and more fruitful.

It makes use of a few simple tools that combine the wisdom of ancient spiritual traditions with the common sense of the twenty-first century.

It explores five aspects of choice-making:

Clearing the decks.
Some choices are far more important than others. Some are not really ours to make. How do we sift the wheat from the chaff?

Starting where you are.
We can only make sound choices from the place we actually find ourselves, not from where we wish we were, or think we ought to be. How do we learn to be true to ourselves?

Reading the signposts.
Life provides us with teachers—
wisdom from outside ourselves, and wisdom from within.
How do we read these signposts?

Choosing for the best.
How do we turn our compromises and collusions
into choices that reflect the very best in us?

Seeing it through.
Making a decision is one thing.
Implementing it is another. What if we make mistakes?
Can we change course if we get things wrong?

This is a book of suggestions, not a rule book.
There is no "answer book" for dealing with life's choices.
In every case we have to work it out for ourselves.
The solutions that work in life are the ones we discover
for ourselves, not the ones we find in the books.

So blend anything you find helpful in these pages
with a large measure of your own experience
and your own life-wisdom.

Wise Choices offers you merely a mixing bowl
and a few spoons,
and the encouragement to trust the processes of your own
heart and mind.

CLEARING
THE DECKS

SHOULD YOU ENGAGE WITH
EVERY CHOICE YOU HAVE?

If you look closely at the way you make your choices,
you may notice certain patterns:

Some issues are important to you. You engage with them
and make your choices about them.

Some issues go beyond your own control.
You have to leave the choices, at least in part, to others.
You delegate the choosing to people you trust
to make choices on your behalf.

Some issues may be important, but also potentially
uncomfortable or even painful. It can be tempting to sweep
the matter under the carpet and hope it will go away.
This avoids the immediate need to make a choice, but it can
mean storing up much more difficult choices for the future.

Some choices are simply not worth spending any
time or energy on.

Before getting too deeply involved with a particular choice,
it's worth looking at where it fits in on this kind of scale.

SORTING THE WHEAT
FROM THE CHAFF

Our choices in life don't all carry equal weight.
But, in practice, we tend to react
to every choice situation with the same basic
"fight or flight" mechanism.
We either throw ourselves into the choosing,
or we duck out of it,
without too much thought about what we are doing.

A quick mental checklist may help you sort out
the wheat from the chaff:

Is this issue worth spending any time or energy on?
If not, let it go
and make space for the things that *do* matter.

Is this choice really up to you,
or is it someone else's responsibility?
Are you wasting your energy
on things you can't change anyway,
or on things beyond your range of influence?
If so, let it go
and make space for things that *are* your responsibility.

When the chaff is cleared,
you should be able to recognize more clearly
the choices you really do need to make,
including, perhaps, a few you might prefer to avoid.

We all need to learn the art of letting go of the things
that are simply
cluttering up our minds unnecessarily.

DOES THIS CHOICE
REALLY MATTER?

How do you decide whether an issue matters to you or not?

This will probably come largely down to intuition,
but a few key questions may be helpful:
Is this issue going to make any real difference to your own
life or the life of anyone else? Will it affect anyone's safety
or well-being?

If the answer to these questions is "No," you still have a
choice about whether to engage with the issue or not.

Next you might ask, "What will happen if I do nothing?"

The consequences of doing nothing
are either acceptable to you or not.
If you don't like the result of doing nothing,
then you *do* need to grapple with the issue. If you are
indifferent about the consequences, you can still choose
whether or not to involve yourself with the issue.

This will depend on your answer to the question,
"Do I have the time, energy, and inclination right now to
make a choice about this matter?"

Let's look at an average example.

It's seven in the evening. You are just relaxing when the phone rings. It's a cold call from someone suggesting that you change your credit card.

Do you want to get involved with this choice at all?

How do our questions help?

First: would your choice make any difference to anyone, affecting their well-being or your own?

Only you can know this. Is it important to you or your family to make some possible savings here, or not?

If your answer is yes,
then this is an issue you should engage with.

If your answer is no,
think about what will happen if you do nothing.

In this case, nothing will happen.
Your credit card arrangements will stay as they are.

But maybe tonight you feel like looking into this matter.
Do you have the time and energy to do the sums right now?
If so, fine. If not, a polite "Thank you, but no thank you"
may be in order.

IS THIS CHOICE REALLY UP TO YOU?

Many of the choices that surround us in life go well beyond our own sphere of influence. They are really a matter of teamwork. We have some input into the decision making, but we also have to delegate many of the choices involved to others.

In the public sphere, we choose our representatives;
we choose whether to protest about certain issues;
we don't choose
the basic rate of income tax
or the level of the government budget.
If we don't like what we get, we can choose our
representatives differently at the next election.

In the family, we choose the town where we want to live
and raise our children,
but we don't choose exactly how that town is run.
If we don't like what we get, we have the choice either to
get involved in local planning and politics, or to move on.

So we make some basic choices ourselves, and
we necessarily leave other choices to people who have the
specialist skills and training to make them on our behalf.

The art is to discern
what we can—and should—be making choices about,
and what we can—and must—leave to others.

ARE YOU TRYING TO
AVOID SOMETHING?

But what about those matters that you can and should be
addressing, but you would much rather not look at?
Issues that may demand courageous decisions,
active interventions,
diplomatic conversations,
or choices that may prove to be costly to you?

Take a deep look at the range of issues that are active for
you right now:

Perhaps a strained relationship with someone
that you really wish you could resolve,
but feel afraid of what might happen if you do?

Perhaps a decision to give away something of your time or
energy or resources, which will cause you a certain
amount of hardship?

Perhaps an impending change of job, or lifestyle, or
partnership that makes you feel apprehensive?

Be honest with yourself.

Is there anything you are trying to avoid?

Usually the fear of what lies ahead may be worse than any pain involved in actually making the decisive move.

For now, simply acknowledge that this matter is, indeed, an issue you need to address.

The following chapters offer you some help in making whatever hard choices need to be made.

STARTING WHERE YOU ARE

BEGINNING AT
SQUARE ONE

Once you have cleared the field of those choices
you really don't need to make at all, there is
room to look at the much more important questions:
the choices that *do* matter,
the choices where your response makes a difference.

Wherever you are going, in any issue,
you have to begin where you actually are, here and now.
This is your starting point, your Square One.

"Square One" means the place where you are really *you*,
knowing how you really feel,
in the circumstances where you actually find yourself.

It does *not* mean:
where you wish you were, or
where you think you ought to be, or
where other people want you to be, or
where you might have been, if only . . .

It's all too easy to make important choices
under the influence of someone else's agenda.

It's even possible to live a whole life
living out someone else's dream,
trying to conform yourself to the kind of person
someone else wants you to be.

You can only make sound choices when you begin from
a place where you feel you are being true to yourself and
true to how you *really* are.

In many ways, life is a game of chance.

Each new day deals us a new set of circumstances and
challenges.
We have to handle whatever that day brings.

Some aspects of the day may move us forward.
Others may drag us right back down again.

The "dice" that determine where we land
seem random and uncaring.
Overnight our fortunes can change. We are caught up
in a flux of uncertainty and unpredictability.

How can we make sensible choices amid such chaos?

Well, one thing we *can* do is to begin from where we are.
In fact, that is the only possible place to begin.

So what does Square One look like?

Square One is where circumstance has placed you.

You may be facing hard choices right now,
or on the brink of making life-changing decisions.

It's worth taking time to reflect on where you are really
starting from.
It may not be quite as random as it feels.
It may be a place that holds gifts for you,
as well as problems,
a place where you will find real resources
for making the haphazard journey through your life's
choices.

Take time to explore your personal Square One.

What "soil" are you growing in?

Where has life planted you?

What gifts does this soil contain, and what drawbacks?

GROWING WHERE YOU ARE PLANTED

Sound decisions are grounded in this soil
—the soil of who you really are and where you
find yourself in life.

This doesn't mean that you can't change anything.
It simply means that this is the starting point.

Your whole life is planted in a particular patch of soil
—your family, your upbringing, your education,
your likes and dislikes, your strengths and weaknesses.

This soil will influence your choices in life,
maybe more than you imagine.
It's a good idea to get to know it better,
to become more aware of what it contains.

The main thing it contains is your potential
to become the unique person you truly are,
the fulfilment of God's dream for you,
and your own deepest dream for yourself.

All that potential is there in your Square One.
You won't find it anywhere else!

THE GROUND OF
ALL YOUR CHOICES

Every choice in life also has its own Square One.

Before you begin to explore the choice itself,
look at where it has its roots.
Here the soil may seem like a set of constraints that limit
your decision.

For example:
the place where you live;
the wider needs of your family and friends;
your abilities, which will determine whether you could do
a particular job or not;
your likes and dislikes, which determine what you really
want to choose.

But in fact these constraints are the same soil that
gives you the resources you need
to make your choice and carry it out.

The soil keeps the plant contained in its circumstances.
The soil also contains the nutrients
that allow the plant to grow.

The riverbanks limit the river's free flow. The riverbanks also give the river the channel through which it can flow to its destination.

DRAWING ON EXPERIENCE

One of the gifts we discover if we dig around at Square One
is the memory of our own experience.

Experience is a great teacher:

It can warn us against going down certain paths
that were not helpful in the past.

It can encourage us to take risks, because in the past
similar choices have led to good results.

It can remind us that, although we have made plenty of
mistakes in the past, we are still alive to tell the tale, and
we may need to risk making mistakes in the future.

Try this little formula to test out new choices and decisions:
Have you ever been in this kind of situation before?
If so, how did you choose to respond at the time?
In the light of this experience, how do you choose to
respond now?

Sometimes we need to break free of the habits and
responses of the past.

Sometimes we can learn from them and build on them.
Only experience can show us the difference.

Look at any particular decision you are dealing with
right now.

Where is your starting point
—your Square One—on this issue?

What are the constraints?

Where do you find yourself in this issue?
Are you beginning from where you truly are,
or are you trying to force yourself into a place where you
think you ought to be?
Are you trying to fit yourself into a pattern that other
people think you ought to fit?
Are you trying to work things out from a place where you
wish you were,
or where you might have been if you had started from
somewhere else?

What does your experience tell you?

Listen inside yourself, and ask yourself,
"Where is the real me in all of this?"

BEWARE OF THE "IF-ONLYS"

Take a long look at any *if-onlys* that may be lurking around:

If only I had followed so-and-so's advice last year . . .
If only I had finished my college course . . .
If only I had been born in another time, another place,
another family . . .

The *if-onlys* are the worst enemies of the present moment
—and the present moment is your best friend in all your
choice making.

If-onlys will rob you of your last ounce of energy and
take you absolutely nowhere.
They will send you off down every imaginable cul-de-sac.
They will leave you feeling frustrated and resentful.

The present moment is the source—the only source—
of all the energy you need to make the next best move.

Start where you are.
And if you have already wandered off down some of those
cul-de-sacs, go back . . . to Square One!

BEWARE OF "WHAT-IFS"

Now take a look at another enemy of the
present moment—the *what-ifs*:

What if I get it all wrong and make things worse?
What if I speak my truth honestly and make enemies?
What if I challenge this situation and put my job at risk?
What if people laugh at me?

The *what-ifs* have two faces.

They can be friends,
helping us recognize our options,
warning us about possible outcomes.

But if we let them bully us,
if we start to fill up with fear in their presence,
they are not friends, but enemies.
Caution is a friend of our decision making.
Undue fear is its enemy.

The difference between reasonable caution and excessive
fear is something we can't work out in our heads,
but we feel it in our gut.

So listen to your gut feelings.
Is there turmoil down there? Is fear taking over?

Just notice your reaction
when the *what-ifs* are getting too powerful.
You can actively choose to give them less power
as you move on in your task of making a choice.

YOU ARE WHAT
YOU CHOOSE

Remember those "connect-the-dots" puzzles
you used to do when you were a child?

At first sight they just looked like a random scattering of
dots. It was impossible to guess what hidden picture
the dots contained.
The picture only began to emerge as you painstakingly
joined up the dots, one at a time, step by step.

Life is something of a connect-the-dots mystery too.
Usually it's impossible to see any meaning in the chaos of
our circumstances,
or any pattern emerging out of the mess of everyday living.

Yet underneath it all, inside it all, a pattern is emerging.
A meaning *is* evolving.

We only see it with hindsight.

Sadly, the pattern is sometimes not recognized until the
funeral service,
when we think back over a person's life,
and notice what kind of unique difference it made.

While we live, we are still picking our way forward,
dot by dot.
The way we make our choices
is the way we connect the dots.
Every choice along the way makes a difference to the
picture that will eventually emerge.

We really want the true picture to emerge
at the end of the day.
This is what we would like to leave behind on
Planet Earth:
a true footprint of our true self.

Maybe even a footprint that will help others find
their own true path in life.

But all we can really influence is where the next line goes.
We can only choose the next dot, and hope that it is
helping to shape the true picture,
and not obscuring it or distorting it.

Is it just a matter of "fingers crossed" and
hope we get it right?

Or is there a sounder guide than blind hope, as we take each next step?

PREPARING THE GROUND

Children's connect-the-dots puzzles are easy to follow.
It's fairly obvious where the next line should go.

It's not like that in the real world.
The next line could go almost anywhere.
So how do we choose?

We don't know—and can't yet imagine—the full picture.
But we do know Square One.
We know at least a bit about who we truly are,
and what we truly value.

This gives us a head start in choosing the next step.

There are some useful tools to help us make each new
choice along the way—
the big decisions and the apparently trivial ones.
Together they are forming and shaping "who we are."

But we begin with a little preparation . . .

Decisions, like other projects, tend to do better when we
prepare for them.
The bigger the decision, the more preparation is needed.

The way you prepare depends a lot on the kind of choice
that is on the agenda.

Some are long-term, and demand a lot of thought.
Some are "instants" that you can't prepare for at all.
Some offer a whole variety of options.
Some offer only two: "Take it or leave it."

Take a look at any choices you are dealing with right now:
Are they long-term, or even life-changing?
Or are they "instants?"
Just to name them to yourself is a good way of beginning
to prepare the ground.

REVIEWING THE OPTIONS

Important decisions require some care.

There are things we can do to prepare ourselves better
to make a good choice.

We can set out the options . . .

It's worth putting them down on paper if you can.
What choices do you actually have in this situation?

Go through them one by one:
Are any of them unrealistic?
Are they impossible for practical reasons?
Are they incompatible with your existing responsibilities
and commitments?
Do they go against the voice of your conscience?

Exclude the unrealistic options from your list.
Now you have a clearer view of what the different
possibilities really are in this matter.

This is the starting point for making your choice.

MAKING SNAP DECISIONS

Snap decisions, instant choices, don't give you the luxury
of time and space to think.
Many of them will be relatively trivial,
and unlikely to take you down entirely new pathways
—but they may have a profound effect
on other people.

How you choose to react to a remark or a situation
may make the kind of difference to someone else
that they never forget,
either in thankfulness or resentment.

We can't prepare for snap decisions.
But when we nurture the habit of being careful about the
bigger things,
the smaller things will begin to follow the same kind of
pattern, though we will be unconscious of this.

The care you expend on your bigger choices will color
your "instants" as well.
When you are true to the best in yourself in the big things,
that same integrity will weave through the small things.

But—beware of any pressure to make snap decisions
in situations that you know
really need more time
and thought.

Better, by far, to resist such pressure than to live with
unwanted consequences that could have been avoided.

READING THE SIGNPOSTS

TUITION, AND INTUITION

Let's assume:

You know what kind of choice or decision you are facing;
you have cleared the field of nonessential factors; and
you feel you are starting from a place where you are
being true to yourself.

How can you move on?

Is there anywhere you can look for guidance?

There are two deep wells of wisdom
available to us all.
We can draw from them deeply and often.

Let's call them

Tuition, and

Intuition.

Tuition is something we are given from outside ourselves.
It comes from our parents and family,
our teachers and colleagues,
our friends and our critics.

All these people play a part in instructing us as to
what to do, how to choose, in particular situations.

Intuition is something that dwells within us.
It is an inner wisdom that prompts us gently about the
right course to pursue,
the better reaction to a situation.
It grows out of the values we hold dear,
the hidden springs of experience,
our hopes, dreams, and desires.

It isn't always rational—it isn't meant to be.
It's the partner of our reasoning mind, not an opponent.

Tuition and intuition can work together to draw us
towards the better outcome, the wiser choice.

WHO ARE YOUR TEACHERS?

Take time to notice the sources of tuition that
help you in your decision making.

Who are your role models, and why?
What values and guidelines did you learn from various
teachers or "wisdom figures" in your life?

These values are probably guiding you more profoundly
than you imagine.
Make an effort to become more aware of them.

Some of the best tuition comes from our critics.
Those who disagree with us will tell us the truth,
without flattery. And truth is a great tutor.

Just as children learn more from their mistakes at school
than from their perfect grades,
so we can learn more from our truthful critics than from
those who only tell us what they know we want to hear.

How do you feel about criticism?
Some of it (but not all!)
may be more helpful than you dare to think.

But not everything we are taught is either good or helpful.

Many people grow up with an image of themselves as an
underachiever, for example, or a misbehaving child.

Unconsciously they take this bit of "teaching" into their
adult decision making. They stay in the role that was once
assigned to them.

They are not starting from where they really are,
but from where someone else—parents, teachers,
employers—once thought they were.

Take a deep look at how *you* see yourself,
and where *your* learned reactions are coming from.

Which do you value, and want to keep?
Which would you like to set aside now, and move beyond?

The choice is yours!

LEARNING FROM OTHERS

A different kind of guidance comes from those who have
faced similar decisions before us.

No two people's experience is ever the same, but even so,
we can share some of the learning curves with each other.

A person who has had to deal with some difficulty
—maybe a specific health problem, or hardship,
layoff, marital breakdown, or financial loss—
will often develop real empathy for others in the
same situation.

Self-help groups show how this works in practice.
The wisdom of the group is greater than the sum of the
wisdom of its individual members.

When we need to choose a new computer or car,
we often ask
friends and colleagues for their recommendations.

Why are we so hesitant to do the same when we are
dealing with more serious matters?

CAN I TRUST MY
ADVISERS?

To seek guidance and advice from each other is simply
a part of what it means to be human,
and part of an interrelated, interdependent web of life.

But . . . how do we know which recommendations
we can trust?
We are swamped with "guidance," telling us what we should
eat, drink, wear, and think. And we know instinctively
that this kind of guidance is unreliable.

Why?

Because it has a hidden (or not-so-hidden) agenda.
It is given with the intention of making us part with
our money,
or of gaining some kind of control over us.

Unfortunately, hidden agendas may lurk in apparently
innocent advice as well.
They are so tricky precisely because they *are* hidden.
Before you act on guidance from outside,
ask yourself,

"Does the person offering me this advice have anything
to gain if I accept it,
or anything to lose if I reject it?"

A "yes" to either should trigger a warning bell.

The only kind of guidance or advice that is truly objective
is that which is offered in genuine freedom of heart.

CAN I TRUST MY INTUITIONS?

We have sources of guidance and wisdom deep within
ourselves, too,
though sometimes we are reluctant to trust them.

You could think of your own intuition as a kind of
inner compass.
If you reflect on it, you will recall times when you have
followed it, and it has served you well.

Most of us know intuitively when we are
being true to ourselves,
and when we are walking paths that don't feel right.

We know when the inner compass is reading true,
when we are doing what feels right for us,
responding to life from our true center.

Take a moment to remember any times when you felt
this was happening.
What was the issue in question at the time?
How did you choose to react?
How did you feel at the time?
What was the outcome?

It's important to notice and remember these times
when we are "living true."
They are like an imprint on our hearts,
a blueprint of how it feels when the inner compass
is registering "true north."

But there are, inevitably, many, many times when the
opposite is true.

We make choices from somewhere that is not the true
center of ourselves.

Perhaps we do something to please someone else,
even though we feel a bit uneasy about it.

Perhaps we act out of fear.
The *what-ifs* bully us into doing less then our best.
The *if-onlys* freeze us into regret, and steal the energy
we need to move on.

Perhaps we let ourselves "go with the flow,"
even though in our hearts we know that "the flow" is going
the wrong way.

Or perhaps we settle for less, for mediocrity,
for the safer option,
even though deep down we want to take the risk of going
for what we really desire.

READING THE
INNER COMPASS

Often the inner compass wobbles!

We notice this because we start
to feel anxious, to sense an inner unrest,
to catch ourselves trying to justify what we are doing,
or looking for someone to blame.

We are human, and we all know how this feels.
Take a moment to recall how such times have been for you.
Don't judge yourself. Such judgment is never helpful.
It focuses your energy in the wrong place—
on yourself, rather than on the matter in hand.

Instead, just notice the pattern of how it feels when your
inner compass is wobbling.
Recognizing the symptoms is a major step towards
overcoming them.

Then, when the compass wobbles in the future,
you will be more aware of what is going on
both in your mind and heart,
more free to choose to act against whatever is causing
the wobbles.

The remembered experience of how it feels
when the compass is registering true north
—and when it is not—
becomes part of your store of inner wisdom.

The more we follow our intuitions when they are
registering true, the easier it gets.

Inner wisdom is a resource that grows with experience.

TRUSTING THE
INNER COMPASS

When you are on a mountainside and the fog descends,
the only way to be sure of finding the right trail
is to use your map and compass.

But, as many climbers have learned to their cost,
we tend to think we know better than the compass.

The compass points one way, but surely, we think, we came
up the path over *there*.
Perhaps there is something wrong with the compass.

And so we rationalize our own faulty memories of where
the path might be.
Or perhaps we talk each other into taking a wrong turn.
And perhaps we end up in the wrong valley—or worse!

When we are making important decisions,
we need to *trust* the inner compass.

It will guide us more surely than our reactions to the
immediate conditions,
or the advice of panicking friends.

LISTENING TO
OUR FEELINGS

What helps us read this mysterious inner compass?

It may surprise you to learn that your feelings
can be your teachers.

Feelings? Such fickle things?
Indeed, they *are* fickle,
but they tell us the truth, nevertheless,
about where we really are at the time.

Imagine a sandy beach.
You want to walk on it safely,
but part of the beach is composed of quicksand.
In other parts there is rock beneath the sand.
The sand looks the same everywhere,
so how do you know where the rock is,
and where the quicksand is?
The answer is usually—
"From experience!"

You learn where the quicksand is
by *feeling* your feet being sucked down,
and the fear that grips you when this happens.

You notice where it is safe to walk
by *feeling* the firm rock supporting your steps.

You won't forget those feelings.
They will be your trustworthy guides,
whenever you walk on the beach.

Life is a bit like that beach.

It is full of hidden hazards,
quicksand that sucks us down into the depths of despair.

But it also has areas of solid rock,
where we know we are on firm ground
and we can walk with confidence.

The key to discovering the nature of the terrain begins
with our *feelings*.

It can be very helpful to cultivate the habit of
reflecting back over the events of the passing days.

It helps us to begin to live *reflectively*.

LIVING REFLECTIVELY

Take time to *reflect back* over how the day has been . . .

What happened to make you feel you were on shaky ground?
Notice any feelings of being inwardly unsteady.
Now notice what gave rise to them.

Perhaps something was said that created a bad atmosphere.
Perhaps you reacted out of fear,
or a false desire to please someone,
and afterwards you felt discontented with yourself,
or uneasy about the outcome of your choice.

These movements are like the quicksand. They are
strong warnings that we are not walking on solid ground.
Notice them—notice where they come from.
Maybe a particular relationship regularly drains you of
energy, or undermines your confidence.
Maybe some issue in your life is filling you with
apprehension.

Just notice these connections.
Your feelings can point to the quicksand in your life,
and help you to avoid the shaky ground in the future.

And what happened during the day to make you feel
you were walking on a solid foundation?

Perhaps you made a choice and felt intuitively that the
right thing had been done or said,
in the right way,
at the right time.

Perhaps events proved that a particular friend is reliable,
or that some activity or task in your life draws out
the best in you and renews your energy,
or that some relationship always leaves you feeling
more alive.

If you make a habit of reflecting back over the day,
you will learn to read the map of your circumstances,
and recognize what regularly tends to suck you down
and what helps to move you on.

Feelings and reflection go together.
Feelings alone will not help you
unless you reflect on what they are telling you.

To listen to your feelings,
and then to reflect on their signals,
is to learn the art of *reflective living.*

Reflection like this only needs to take a few minutes,
but it can make a big difference to your ability
to make wise choices.

NOTICING ANY
OVERREACTIONS

Overreactions are another very sound guide to what is
really going on in your heart.

Did you go over the top about anything during the day?
What triggered the reaction?
How do you feel about it in hindsight?

An overreaction like this
is like the bubbles from a submerged shark.
It is a telltale sign that something bigger is lurking
under the surface of what you see.

If you notice bubbles like this coming up in your day,
it may be very important to stop at that point
and ask yourself—without judgment!—
where are these bubbles really coming from?

If you lost your temper with a colleague,
or grumbled at the neighbor's children,
or you came close to road rage with another driver,
where was this negative energy coming from?

Very often you will find that it isn't all it seems to be.

The driver who enrages you may actually be activating
deeper reasons for your anger.

The girl who delays you in the supermarket,
by chatting needlessly to the person in front of you,
may actually be doing you a favor.
She may be the signal that warns you
that the pressures in your life are running dangerously high.

THE GIFT OF
LIFE'S IRRITATIONS

Life is full of minor and major irritations.
The irritant can be a pain—but the pain itself can be
the symptom of something more seriously wrong.

Pain is in some ways a blessing.
It is the body's early warning system that
something is wrong, and needs attention,
before it becomes a threat to health and life.

The irritants that get under our skin,
and make us overreact,
can be blessings too.
They can be our inner early warning system
that something needs attention,
before it threatens our inner well-being,
our relationships,
or even our integrity.

The grit in the oyster
is the irritant that becomes the pearl.

Don't disregard the irritants of your daily life.
They may have the makings of precious pearls of wisdom.

THE GIFT OF DESIRE

An especially potent feeling is the feeling of *desire*.

The word "desire" is charged with meaning.
What does it mean to *you*?

Desire has a bad press.
We tend to think that if we desire something,
it is probably something we ought not to want or to have.

But think about it:
Without desire we would never get up in the morning.
We would never have ventured beyond our own front door.
We would never have read a book or learned anything new.

No desire means no life, no growth, no change.
Desire is what makes two people create a third person.
Desire is what makes the crocuses push up through the late
winter soil.

Desire is energy,
the energy of all creativity, the energy of life itself.

So, let's not be too hard on desire.

WHAT DO YOU
"REALLY" WANT?

Can our desires help us to make wise choices?

It depends on how deep they go.

There are deep desires,
and there are shallow desires.

Shallow desires translate into wish lists.
They turn up for holidays and birthdays.
We would like to have this, that, and the next thing.
We could probably live happily without these things,
but if we are asked what we want,
we can usually supply a list.

If your children or friends were to ask you,
"What would you like for your birthday?"
—what would you say?
Just notice these wants and wishes.
Notice how deeply you feel about them.
What sacrifices would you be willing to make
in order to gain what you want?

Now take a look at a deeper level of desiring:
Is there something you have always wanted to do, but
never managed? What are your unfinished dreams?
If you had your life over again, what would you change?
If you had only a few months to live,
how would you use the time?
If a significant sum of money suddenly came your way,
how would you spend it?
If you were granted three wishes, what would they be?
Is there anyone, or anything, you would literally
give your life for?

Take time to ponder one or more of these questions.
The responses you make to yourself
—provided they are your honest answers,
and not just the answers you feel you *ought* to give—
will be pointers to where your deepest desires are rooted.

Look closely, taking time to reflect on what you find.
There may be patterns in your desiring that help you
understand more fully who you are.

Sometimes our apparently superficial desires can lead us
down to the deeper levels.

For example, a friend tells you that he wants a garden.
"Why is that?" you might ask.

Given the opportunity, your friend might begin
to unpack the reasons:
To have a real break from work on the weekends . . .
To have an oasis of peace in life . . .
To have fresh flowers and vegetables . . .
To have a place where one could spend quality time with
family and friends . . .

So, this desire isn't just a self-centered "I want!"

It has to do with deeper issues, such as:
A desire for peace, and a return to a more tranquil life.
A desire to deepen and nourish important relationships.
A desire to counteract the effects of stress.

These are deeper layers of desiring.

How do they affect the way we make our choices?

Well, these deeper layers are always there,
unconsciously affecting the way we shape our lives.

Any choices we make that *go against* our deep desires
will leave us feeling uneasy and discontented.

The choices we make that *nourish* these deep desires
will leave us feeling more in harmony with ourselves and
those we love.

The deep desires
affect the smaller choices,
in ways we may not always realize.

It matters to recognize the shape of our deep desires.
It helps us to make our everyday choices
in ways that align with these deep desires and values.

And ultimately, we will find inner peace most readily
if our own deep desires and values
are in harmony, and not at odds, with
the deep desires, hopes, and aspirations
of the whole human family,
and of all creation.

CHOOSING FOR
THE BEST

NAVIGATING LIFE'S SHIFTING SEAS

We've looked at the sources of wisdom and experience that
help us make our decisions.

These provide signposts that we need in all our
decision making.
They are wells that nourish our ability to choose wisely,
and from which we can draw freely.

As we grow in self-awareness,
welcoming respectfully all that life has to teach us,
through history and through each other,
and learning to trust our own inner compass,
we become more and more equipped
to face the choices with which life confronts us,
and to navigate the shifting winds and currents of our
everyday living.

We may not have any choice about the random events that toss us, day by day, back and forth between "smooth sailing" and "rough seas."

Some choices we face seem to offer us the benefit of favorable winds.
Things are looking good. Chance has thrown us a golden opportunity. All we need to do is sail with the wind.

In other situations the opposite is true. Adverse winds threaten to pull us off course, dragging us to places where we never intended to go.

And sometimes a particular choice we face brings both these possibilities at once—risk and opportunity, danger as well as the chance to grow.

We have no choice about where circumstances cast us.
But we *do* have a choice about whether we go
with the wind,
or steer against it.

SAILING WITH THE WIND

A "favorable wind" is a way of describing
all those situations
that invite you to live true to who you really are.
Favorable winds or currents in your life draw you on
to search for your personal best,
to make the wise choices that will make a difference,
not just for yourself, but for others.

These favorable winds and currents ask you,
"What does the *best* in you choose to do?"

This may not be the *easiest* option.
You still need to set your course
resolutely and confidently
towards the beckoning Best.

Often it would be much easier just to drift along
with the day's routine and let the opportunity pass you by.

But if you can seize the moment,
you won't regret it.
The best in you will grow stronger.
It will be easier to choose the better course next time.

You will do this best if you know
where you are most likely to encounter
the favorable winds and currents in your life.

Take some time to reflect on any situations,
or relationships, activities, times, or places,
that consistently draw out the best in you.
Name them to yourself.
Acknowledge their benevolent influence on you,
and reaffirm to yourself
the desire to be in partnership with them.

What might you do, specifically, to focus your energy
on the things that nourish the best in you,
to overcome any reluctance you may detect in yourself,
and to make the effort to steer the boat of your life
in the direction of the better course?

Next time you are facing a decision, ask yourself,
"Is my choice in this matter drawing out the best in me?"

NAVIGATING THE NEGATIVES

The negative winds and currents in your life's ocean
are those situations that lead you away from the best
in yourself—they are the seductive movements that
distract you and steal the energy you really need
to keep growing into the person you truly are.

The power of these negative movements
can pull you off course
or suck you down to the depths
faster than you may think.

It takes no effort at all
to be swept away by currents like these.
Once you are in their grip
it is hard to pull yourself back to a true course,
whether you are at sea in a boat, or
struggling with the demands of the voyage of life.

To avoid this downward drag,
you may have to deliberately act against its force.

You can do this best when you are familiar with the nature
of these treacherous currents or malicious winds,

when you are aware of where they tend to show themselves,
and where you are personally most vulnerable to them.

So take time, and keep on taking time,
to reflect on what these harmful winds and currents mean
for you.
Are there any situations, or relationships,
or activities, or times, or places,
where you know, from experience,
that you are likely to be pulled away
from your personal truth,
and make choices that are not worthy of the best in you?

Is there something you can do
to work actively against the effects of these influences
that are pulling you away from your heart's true course?

Look at any choices you are facing.
Are any negative currents affecting your decision?
What might you do to counteract their power?

CHOOSING THE BETTER

Favorable opportunities are not always simply good news.
Sometimes they are merely the least harmful of several
options, and we have to choose "the lesser of two evils."
To choose well is to choose the best we can.

Negative influences are not always simply bad news.
Often, in real life,
they are just the "less good."
Often the choice lies between the good and the better.
The good can sometimes be the enemy of the better.
To choose well is to choose the better.

Maybe you are trying even now
to navigate your way through waters that offer you
good sailing
as well as unseen dangerous currents.

Look closely at this particular situation,
this specific choice before you.
Name the positive elements in it,
and name the negatives.

What shape do they take?
What kind of distraction or temptation
is this harmful current about?
What kind of opportunity or challenge
is this favorable wind about?

Which will you choose?
Which way will you steer your boat?
How will the *best* in you choose?

LISTENING TO
PAST EXPERIENCE

Take a trip through your memory bank.
Where, in your previous experience,
has this particular destructive current,
this form of distraction or temptation led you?

Is that where you want to go now?

Where, in your previous experience,
has this kind of supportive current,
this kind of challenge or opportunity led you?

Is this where you want to go now?

If you knew you only had a short time to live,
which way would you choose?

Remember, from your own experience,
how the supportive currents give you energy.
They have the potential to make you more alive,
more truly who you are
—but you have to cooperate with them,
steer your course by them.

The destructive currents will take you for all you've got!
They have the potential to deaden you
and impede your growth into who you truly are.
They can pull you off course faster than you know.
But you have the choice
about whether to sail with them
or work against them.

SOME KILLER CURRENTS

Be alert especially for these common,
and treacherous, currents:

False programming that tells you
you are no good . . .
you'll never manage it . . .
you'll never keep it up . . .
you just haven't got it in you.

You may have been programmed like this as a child,
but you are not a computer.
You don't have to keep running this program.
You have a choice.

False securities that tell you
it's too risky . . .
they might laugh . . .
earn enough, own enough, and you'll be fine . . .
if you build enough defenses, you will be invulnerable.

But external defenses won't protect you.
Only your inner resources will give you solid ground.

False expectations that
this new job, or this new relationship, or this new house,
will solve everything.

At the end of the day,
both the problem
and the solution
lie in your own hands,
and your own choices.

TESTING YOUR CHOICES

There are some practical tools to help you check out your
choices before doing anything irrevocable.

Let's look at a few of them:
the "ripple effect" test;
the "pros and cons" test;
the "dry run" test;
and the "barometer" test.

THE "RIPPLE EFFECT" TEST

No one is an island.
What one person decides affects many others.
What you decide may cast ripples right across
the world's pond.
It may decisively affect people you don't even know,
even people not yet born,
and the planet those people will inhabit.

Take a look at the choice you are making.
As far as you are able to predict,
what effect might it have on you?

And on those close to you?
Children, partners, parents,
friends, colleagues, neighbors?

What effect might it have on the wider population?
On your neighborhood, your workplace,
your community, the rest of the world?

What effect might it have on creation as a whole?
On the planet, and all its creatures, and on generations
still unborn?

THE "PROS AND CONS" TEST

For this exercise you will need paper and a pencil.
If your choice affects other people directly,
you might want to do the exercise together.

Look at the various, realistic, options you have identified
for this decision.

For each option, use a sheet of paper,
divided down the middle.
On one side, list all the advantages of choosing
in favor of this option.
On the other side, list all the disadvantages.

Repeat the process for each of your options.

At the end of the exercise, you will have a clearer picture
of which option is the more favorable.

If more than one person is involved, this will also reveal
the genuine desires and needs of the individuals concerned.

THE "DRY RUN" TEST

Give yourself enough time and space to "live with" the
alternative scenarios of your decision in your imagination.
"Enough time" means at least a couple of days,
more if necessary.

Say to yourself, I have firmly decided to do A.
Let the days take their course, as if Course A were
fixed and settled.
How do you feel about the consequences of choosing
Course A?
Is your inner compass registering true, or is it wobbling?
Notice especially any feelings of unease or tension
—these might be signs that Course A is not for you.
Notice any feelings of inner peace, even joy
—these might be suggesting that Course A is just right.

Now change over. Do the same for Course B,
and for any further possibilities you have in mind.
Note down how you are feeling, in each case,
especially any thoughts or feelings
that seem to be warning you
of possible unwanted consequences.

So far, this is still just in your mind.

You haven't committed yourself to either of the options.

Let your own feelings and reactions be your guide.

THE "BAROMETER" TEST

Look at the choice you are trying to make, and the direction your decision appears to be going.

Suppose you could measure the quality of your choice on a barometer.

At the top of the scale is what the best in you would choose.

At the bottom of the scale is what the worst in you would choose.

On a scale of one to ten, where do you think your preferred choice would register on this barometer? Be completely honest with yourself.

How do you feel about your assessment? Are there any adjustments you would want to make to your decision now?

Remember that it isn't always realistically possible to choose the very best we would want to choose. Don't be hard on yourself, but be honest!

OTHER TECHNIQUES

A few other techniques can also help you to test your
choices in advance:

Ask yourself how you would choose if you had only
a short time to live.
It is said that the closer we approach the ultimate threshold,
the more clearly we focus on what really matters to us.
What really matters to you in this choice?

Ask yourself how you would advise someone you love,
if they were facing the choice that lies before you.
What might you want to say to this person, and why?

Think of the person in your life whose opinion and values
you most genuinely admire.
How do you think this person would advise you?

Remember, quite consciously, any times in the past when
you have faced a similar kind of choice.
How did you choose then?
How do you feel today about that choice in the past?
How does the experience affect the way you want to make
your choice now?

HAVE YOU DRAWN A COMPLETE BLANK?

It has been wisely noted that when you are trying to decide between A and B, sometimes X is the answer.

Do you feel totally stuck?
Do you really not know at all which option to go for?
Does every possible path leave you feeling confused and unsure of yourself?

This may be an indication that none of the possibilities you have identified is the right course to follow.

Try letting them all go, and living for a day or two with the blank space they leave behind.

Just let things be.
Try to not even think about the problem,
but to keep your mind alert and open. It may be that a very different course of action suggests itself to you, maybe something you had never even considered.

If so, try putting this new option through the discernment tests—and see what happens.

CAN YOU GET IT
WRONG?

Of course we can get things wrong.
We are human.
To err is human.
The more we err, the more human we are!

If success means the perfect immediate solution for all
concerned,
then most of the time we will fail.

But if success means becoming daily more true
to who we really are,
then actually we cannot fail.

Every time we choose what the best in us desires,
we grow a little bit closer to that "best."

Every time we make an unwise choice,
we enter into what is potentially
a new learning curve.

LEARNING FROM
THE MISTAKES

Like children,
we learn more from our mistakes
than from our perfect solutions.

Like creation,
we evolve through difficulty and challenge,
not through the easy times
when there is nothing to stretch us.

Why do we so rarely learn from our mistakes?
Perhaps it is because we never admit that they are
our mistakes.
We prefer to blame someone else,
or our upbringing,
or simply "them."

To own our mistakes
is to embrace our own potential
to grow better, wiser,
and more fully human.

BECOMING WHAT
WE CHOOSE

There is a creative dynamic at work in us,
constantly striving to weave something new and better
out of whatever we present,
growing our poor into better, and our good into best.
We can choose to work with it or against it,
but we can't opt out of it.
It is the dynamic of life
in an evolving universe.

But the opposite dynamic is also in evidence.
It is constantly striving
to pull our best down to mediocre
and our poor to worst.
We see its footprints in history,
and we know where it can lead.
We can choose to let it pull us out of our true orbit,
or we can choose to act against it.

It is our choices that make us who we are.
And in an evolving universe,
our choices make a difference
for all creation.

The ocean is bigger than our "boat,"
and our personal efforts to navigate
the harmful and the helpful currents
are part of something much, much larger.
Just a part,
but a unique and essential part.

And sometimes a harmful current
that sweeps us wildly off course
may deliver us to new waters,
a fresh starting place,
open up a new angle on a problem
we thought we couldn't solve.

SEEING IT
THROUGH

IMPLEMENTING
YOUR CHOICES

To give a good talk, one needs about twenty times as long
to prepare as to deliver it.

The same is true when making choices. The time to prepare
a decision may far exceed the time it takes to implement it.

Even so, the hardest part of giving a talk
is actually standing there and giving it.

The hardest part of making a choice
is actually putting it into practice.

Now you have weighed all the options,
you have done all you can to check out the likely outcome
of your choice,
you have taken account of all the wisdom available to you,
you have listened to your own gut feelings, your intuitions,
your inner compass.

You have reached a conclusion.

What has to happen to make it a reality?

OVERCOMING INERTIA

The first step is the hardest.

For most people, much of the time,
getting a new project off the ground,
or making a change to how we are living or behaving,
or getting down to fixing a long-standing problem,
can feel like a task that grows bigger and more
difficult with every day that we delay it.

Look at the choice you are trying to implement.
What is that crucial first step about?
What makes it seem so difficult?

Name any fears you have.
Identify any actual obstacles that stand
between your decision and its implementation.

Procrastination is a subtle enemy of our best intentions.
Is there something you can do, today,
to get started on putting your decision into effect?

ONE STEP AT A TIME

The main reason why so many of our good resolutions
appear to come to nothing
is because we try to do too much, too soon.

Faced, for example, with the chaos of a cluttered
household, or an overfilled schedule,
or an overwhelming list of things to do,
we can drown in despair of ever setting our lives to rights.
A good way to begin is to do just one small task—
to tidy up just one corner of one room,
to write just one letter, or make one decisive phone call.

In this way we can begin to clear the clutter
from our mental landscape.
Each one thing we do will make the remainder a little bit
more manageable.

Look again at the decision you are trying to implement:
Try breaking down the task ahead of you
into a series of smaller steps
that you might take, one at a time,
over the days and weeks ahead.

Is there just one thing you can do immediately
to begin the process of making your decision a reality?

Taking control of the task like this
will rob it of its power to overwhelm
and intimidate you.

TRUST YOURSELF

Self-doubt is a major culprit
when it comes to undermining your resolve
to implement your decisions.

If doubts are causing you to hold back
and waver on the threshold of decisive action,
remember that you have already been through a process
of serious discernment on this matter.
You have considered your options.
You have weighed the pros and cons.
You have reflected on the effects of your decision
on yourself, and on others.
You have listened to the voice of your own intuition,
and the voices of wise guides and mentors.

You have come to a reasoned and informed decision.

Yet your confidence in this process and in yourself
is wavering.
What can you do?

FACING DOUBTS

Look again at your decision
and at what needs to happen now
to put it into effect.

What is the nature of your doubts?

Are they centered on the wisdom of this particular
decision? Do you feel you need to go
through the discernment process again,
in whole or in part?

If you have serious doubts,
don't hesitate to think again before you act.
Better, by far, to postpone a major life decision
—like marriage, or having a child, or changing your job—
than to live with regret and recrimination in the future.

Or is this really a crisis of confidence in yourself
and your own ability to direct the course of your own life
in ways that reflect your deepest dreams
and sincere desires?

Are you really questioning your decision, or yourself?

Is this a recurring pattern in your life?
What has helped you in the past
to trust your own judgment?
What can you learn from your past experience of events
that proved it was wise to trust yourself,
and from instances
when your judgment let you down?
How do these memories help you now?

What can you do to build the necessary confidence
in yourself?
A trusted friend or mentor can be the catalyst you need
to help you move beyond self-doubt to self-confidence.

TAKING RISKS

Most of the important decisions in our lives
carry considerable risk.
None of us can predict the future.
No one really knows in advance
how a personal relationship will grow, or shrivel,
through the years.
No one can foresee whether a job opportunity
will lead to fulfillment or disaster.

How hard is it for you personally
to take risks?
Do you relish, or dread, the thought of living dangerously?

We can't change our personalities,
but we can learn to make and implement our decisions
in ways that *reflect* our personalities,
rather than trying to work *against* them.

If you find it hard to take risks,
then start with small and careful steps,
risking a little,
allowing each new situation to challenge you
a little way beyond your comfort zone,

sufficiently to let you grow a little,
without breaking you and shattering your fragile
confidence.

If you are a natural risk-taker,
then seize the moment,
but maybe let each new decision
challenge you to also pause and reflect,
modifying your more impetuous tendencies
and drawing you into a more measured wisdom.

Whatever your personality,
life will send you constant invitations to grow.
We grow by taking the chances that life brings
according to the best wisdom we have.
If we don't grow, we die.

HARD CHOICES

It may be that hard moves are needed,
or hard words,
or hard feelings.

Maybe a draining—or even abusive—relationship
has to be ended.
People will get hurt.

Maybe a dependent person has to be liberated
from such dependency,
and maybe that person won't welcome the liberation at all.

Maybe the voice of truth has to be heard
where there is deceit,
and maybe that will cost
what appears to be a good job,
a good reputation,
a comfortable life.

Or maybe past harm needs to be undone,
and apologies or reparations are called for,
and humility, and the ability to start over again.

These are not easy places to be,
but they are human places,
and they are places of great growth.

Two very human qualities may be needed,
in careful balance with each other.

The first is *honesty*, integrity,
being true to who you really are.

The second is *empathy*, compassion,
being sensitive to who the other person really is.

How will you implement your choice,
holding these two qualities in balance?

Look at your choice now in this light.
What has to happen to make it real?
Are you ready to meet the cost?

To be human—really human—is costly,
but it is always worth the price.

CAN YOU CHANGE
YOUR MIND?

Life moves on.
Nothing is fixed.
Sometimes it is necessary to change your mind.
And sometimes it might be the worst possible thing to do.

How can you tell?

To change your mind about a wrong decision
is a sign of honesty.
It reveals the healthy humility of someone who has the
grace to know
that they are not always right,
and the courage to admit it to others.

If you are experiencing regrets
about a choice you have made in your life,
how do you know whether you should reverse it,
assuming that reversal is still possible?

CHANGING COURSE

First look at the nature of your regrets.

Are they about the actual choice you made?
Do you feel, now, that you genuinely chose the
wrong course of action?
What are your reasons for feeling like this?

Have the consequences been harmful for yourself,
or for others? Has the choice you made not led to the result
you were hoping for?

Now ask yourself whether you *can* still change your choice.

If you change the course of action you actually
implemented, how would this affect other people?
Would it undermine your existing commitments?
Would anyone benefit from your change of course?
And who would suffer from it?

If you do change course, don't do so in haste.
Take time to go through the discernment process again.
Talk it through with anyone who is affected by it, and listen
to their feelings.

Or are your regrets
more to do with the cost of implementing
your choice?

Perhaps you feel it has all proved to be much harder work
than you expected?
Or maybe, after all, you can't bring yourself to make the
hard decisions needed to implement your choice?

What truly lies beneath your desire to change your mind?

Is it, deep down, about a lack of courage in yourself?
Is it fear of failure?
Or is it about the demands of compassion for others?

Look back to how you really felt
when you made the decision.

Was your inner compass registering true north?
In your innermost heart,

did you feel that this was the
right thing to do?

If so, don't go back on a decision you took
when you felt you were really being true to the best
in yourself,
now that your inner compass is starting to waver.

The choices we make when we are being most true
to ourselves
should not be reversed simply because we hit times of
challenge and difficulty, doubt and bewilderment.

If you chose this course when your inner eyes
were seeing clearly,
don't change course simply because the fog has descended.
It isn't good navigation when you are at sea in a boat.
It isn't wise when you are at sea in your life.

Stay true to a course that you chose when your
inner compass
was giving you a true reading.

On the other hand,

if you made a bad choice,

at a time when your inner eyes were clouded

and your vision wasn't clear,

then it may be necessary to make a change—

if your existing commitments allow it,

if no one will be harmed by it,

and *if* you have the courage to do it.

Before you reverse a choice you once made,
look long and hard
at what is prompting you to change your mind.

Is the nudge coming from a good place—for example,
a desire to improve things,
a desire to be more honest,
a desire to put right any harm that may have been done?

Or is it coming from a bad place—such as
fear,
resentment or revenge,
a tendency to vacillate?

The same wisdom applies now as for your original choice.

What does the *best* in you choose to do?

A trusted friend can be a helpful mentor in trying to
discern just what the best in you *really* chooses.

Share your feelings—the good and the bad—
and as you talk things through,
you may hear your own true voice,
and your friend may be able to reflect the echo of that
true voice back to you,
and help you to listen to its wisdom.

MOVING ON

Our choices in life become companions
we have to live with.

It is liberating to realize that what is in the past
cannot be changed.

You may go back to the same river again and again,
but you will never see the same water.

You may revisit old choices over and over,
but you can never relive that bit of your history.

Time moves on, and we move with it.

The only thing we can change is the future.

So don't let your life be taken over
by the *what-ifs*,
the *if-onlys*,
and the *might-have-beens*.

You need all your energy
to choose the way ahead.

The freedom to move on
means letting go of everything that holds us captive to
the past.

It also means accepting the consequences of whatever
decisions we have made.

Decisions can go wrong . . .

We can waste a lot of energy,
needlessly berating ourselves,
or wrongly blaming others, or circumstances,
for choices that we made ourselves.

This route only leads to reproaches and recriminations,
weariness and war,
war within ourselves or against the world.
It never leads to life.

Real freedom lies in the realization
that what is past cannot be changed.

Such freedom gives us the space
to focus on what lies ahead,

changing what we can change,
accepting what we can not,
and seeking always the wisdom to know the difference,

and remembering that in everything we do,
at every fork in the road of our journey through life,
however large or small,
we have a choice.

The choice is always about "which way *forward*,"
and it always begins right where we are.